Italian:

Learn Italian in 21 DAYS!

A Practical Guide To Make Italian Look Easy! EVEN For Beginners

Table Of Contents

Introduction

This book contains **21 highly-instructive chapters** on the fundamentals of Italian grammar and communication strategically developed to respond to the needs of travellers, professionals, business owners, students, and self-learners for a learning material that will help them speak the language fluently and confidently in a few weeks time.

It offers a comprehensive yet straightforward discussion of the essential aspects of Italian grammar and provides the tools to help accelerate learning, enhance comprehension, and increase retention. It aims to provide a complete resource for students and language enthusiasts who prefer to learn the language at their own pace.

The first chapters are devoted to learning the basics: pronunciation, numbers, months, days, years, telling time, colors, and useful phrases for different occasions and daily conversations. The succeeding chapters provide an intensive discussion of grammar rules that new and intermediate students should know by heart to be able to communicate successfully in Italian.

Every chapter provides learning aids, charts, tables, and examples to make learning as easy as possible. The final chapter provides a listing of useful Italian terms.

Chapter 1: The Italian Alphabet

There are twenty-one letters in the Italian base alphabet and five additional letters for words of foreign origin (j, k, w, x, and y).

Letter	Letter Name	Letter Sound
A,a	a	AH
B,b	bi	BEE
C,c	ci	CHEE
D,d	di	DEE
E,e	e	AY
F,f	effe	EF-FAY
G,g	gi	JEE
H,h	acca	AHK-KA
I,i	i	EE
L,l	elle	EL-LAY
M,m	emme	EM-MAY
N,n	enne	EN-NAY
O,o	o	OH
P,p	pi	PEE
Q,q	cu	COO
R,r	erre	AIR-RAY
S,s	esse	ES-SAY
T,t	ti	TEE
U,u	u	OO
V,v	vu (or vi)	VOO (or) VEE
Z,z	zeta	ZAY-TAH

Additional letters

Letter	Pronunciation	Name	Letter Sound	English Sound
j	English pronunciation	i lunga	EE LOON-GA	jump
k	English pronunciation	cappa	KAH-PAH	crack
w	English pronunciation	doppia vu	DOPE-PEE-AH VOO	well
x	English pronunciation	ics	EEX	examine
y	English pronunciation	ipsilon	EEP-SEE-LONE	yes

Chapter 2: Pronunciation Guide

Italian is a romance language that is relatively easy to learn. A phonetic language, Italian words are usually spoken as they are written. This section is devoted to the essential aspects of Italian pronunciation. You will learn how each letter is pronounced individually and in combination with other letters. You will be introduced to stress and accent marks as well as elision, which are indispensable in spoken Italian.

The Vowel Sounds

Italian vowels are short and sharp and should not be slurred. There are 5 vowels but 7 vowel sounds. The vowels "a", "i", and "u" are always pronounced in the same manner while "e" and "o" are pronounced in two ways: open and closed. The pronunciation is always open when the vowel is stressed and it is closed when the vowel is unstressed.

Vowel Sounds

Vowel Sound		English Sound	Examples
a		long like a in "father"	amore (love), sala (hall)
e	open	like e in pet	bene (well), bello (beautiful)
	closed	like a in pain	bere (to drink), fede (faith)
i		like ee in meet	pino (pine), libro (book)
o	open	like o in cost	posta (mail), moda (fashion)
	closed	like o in boat	sole (sun), nome (name)
u		like oo in boot	uno (one), lungo (long)

Dipthongs (Dittonghi)

Dipthongs are two vowels that combine to create a single sound. Theoretically, Italian vowels are intended to be pronounced individually. The swiftness of speech, however, tend to result in dipthongs and glides in unaccented vowels.

ai, ae	like 'i' in "eye"	bailare bahy-lah-ray (to dance)
ao, au	like the "ow" in "cow"	auto AHW-toh (car)
ei	like 'ay' in "say"	sei sAHY-ee (six)
eu	like the 'eu' similar in the Spanish "Europa"	pleurite (pleurisy)
ia	like "yah"	bianco bYAHn-koh (white)
ie	like "ye" in yes	lieto lYEH-toh (happy)
io	like "yo"	fiore fYOH-reh (flower)
iu	like "yoo" or the 'ew' in "few"	piu YOO (more)
oi	like 'oy' in "toy"	poi pOY (then,later)
uo	like the 'wo' in "won't"	nuovo nWOH-voh (new)

Tripthongs (Trittonghi)

A tripthong is a sequence of three vowels with one sound. Tripthongs are usually a combination of a dipthong and an unstressed "i" at the end.

Examples:

miei	mYEY	mine
tuoi	tWOY	yours
suoi	sWOY	his
buoi	bWOY	oxen

Consonants (Consonanti)

Sound	English Sound		Examples
b	pronounced like the English sound		
c	before a, o, u	like the "k" in car	culla (cradle), così (so)
	before e or i	like the "ch" in chest	cena (supper), aceto (vinegar)
d	like the English "d" but harsher and more explosive but no puff of air or aspiration		denaro (money), data (date)
f	pronounced like the English sound		
g	before a, o, u	like the "g" in garbage	gomma (eraser), grande (great)
	before e or i	like the "j" in jog	gente (people), pagina (page)
h	always silent		ho (I have), hotel (hotel)
l	similar to "l" in like but sharper		olio (oil), luna (moon)
m	pronounced like the		

	English sound	
n	pronounced like the English sound	
p	like the English sound but pronounced without aspiration	pasto (meal), ponte (bridge)
q	always comes before "u" and the combination is pronounced like the "qu" in quest	questo (this), quadro (picture)
r	a trilled "r"	ora (now), orologio (watch)
s	before b,d,g,l,m,n,r, and v and between vowels, like the "z" in zoo	casa (house), francese (French)
	in other cases, like the "s" in sun	tesoro (treasure), susina (plum)
t	approximates the English "t" sound without escaping a breath	testa (head), contento (glad)
v	pronounced like the English sound	
z	in some cases, voiced like the "ds" in beds	pranzo (lunch), zebra (zebra)
	sometimes, voices like the "ts" in assets	negozio(store), pizza (pizza)

Consonantic Digraphs

Consonantic digraphs are consonant combinations that create a single sound. Following are digraphs in Italian:

gh	always followed by "e" or "i", sounds like the "g" in go	maghi mah-GEE (magicians)
gli	approximates the "ll" in millions	famiglia fah-mee-Lyah (family)
gn	approximates the "ny" in canyon	bagno bah-NYO (bath)
ch	always followed by "e" or "i", sounds like the "k" in kite	perché payr-Kay (because)
sc	before a, o, u like "sk" in ask	pesca pay-Skah (peach)
	before e or i like "sh" in shell	pesce pay-Shay (fish)
sch	always followed by "e" or "i", sounds like the English "sk"	fiaschi fee-yah-Skee (flasks)

Double Consonants

Except for the letters "h" and "q", all Italian consonants can be doubled to create a stronger, prolonged sound. In the case of a double "s", it is unvoiced. A double "z", has no effect at all. Doubling the consonants b, c, d, g, p, or t creates a stronger stop while doubling the consonants f, l, m, n, r, s, or v results in a prolonged sound.

Here are words with double consonants:

albicocca	ahl-bee-koK-Kah	apricot
anno	ahN-Noh	year
babbo	bahB-Boh	dad
basso	bahS-Soh	short
bello	behL-Loh	beautiful
bistecca	bees-tayK-Kah	beef steak
cavalletto	kah-vahL-LayT-Toh	easel
espresso	ays-prehS-Soh	espresso coffee
evviva	ayV-Vee-vah	hurrah
ferro	fehR-Roh	iron
fetta	fayT-Tah	slice
mamma	mahM-Mah	mama
pennello	payn-nehL-Loh	paint brush
ragazzo	rah-gahT-TSO	boy
spaghetti	Spah-ghayT-Tee	spaghetti
tavolozza	tah-voh-loT-Tsah	palette

Stress and Accent Marks

In Italian, only the vowels have stress marks and the accent or stress usually falls on the penultimate syllable. There are however, many exceptions. When the accent is on the last syllable, the vowel is marked with an accent.

The acute accent (é, ó) or accento acuto are used to indicate stress on closed vowels while the grave accent (à, è, ì, ò, ù) is used to indicate stress on open vowels. There are many instances, however, that closed vowels are marked with a grave accent. The grave accent (`) can be found over all vowels but the acute accent (´) may only be found in "e" and "o".

Here are examples of Italian words which are stressed on the penultimate syllable:

padre	PAH-dray	father
uomo	WO-moh	man
nipote	nee-POH-tay	nephew
telefonare	tay-lay-fo-NAH-ray	telephone
parlare	pahr-LAH-ray	to speak
studiare	stu-DYAH-ray	to study
foglia	FOH-lyah	leaf
signorina	see-nyoh-REE-nah	Miss
amico	ah-MEE-ko	friend
Milano	mee-LAH-no	Milan

Words with accent on the last syllable:

An accent is required if the stress falls on the final syllable. Failure to place the stress can lead to misunderstanding in cases where there are similarly spelled words with different meaning.

Here are words with an accent mark on the final syllable:

città	cheet-TAH	city
caffè	kahf-FEH	coffee
però	peh-ROH	but
tassì	tahs-SEE	taxi
lunedì	loo-neh-DEE	Monday
venerdì	vay-nayr-DEE	Friday
perché	pehr-KEY	why, because
cioè	chow-EH	namely
virtù	veer-TOO	virtue

In some instances, similarly-spelled words are distinguished only by the placement of an accent mark.

regìa	rehjyhah	direction of a movie /play
règia	rehjah"	royal
àncora	ahnkohrah	anchor
ancòra	ahnkohrah	again, more
lavàti	lahvahtih	washed
làvati	lahvahtih	wash yourself
capitàno	kahpytahnoh	captain
càpitano	kahpytahnoh	they happen
là	LAH	there
la	LAH	the/ it/ her

14

dà	DAH	gives
da	DAH	from
è	AY	is
e	EH	and
sé	SEH	himself/herself
se	SAY	if
sì	SEE	yes
si	SEE	oneself
ne	NAY	some
né	**NEH**	**nor**

Several words ending with –che (pronounced as KAY) are written with an accent on the last vowel.

giacché	jahk-KAY	since
perché	payr-KAY	why, because
benché	bayng-KAY	despite
poiché	pohy-KAY	because
sicché	seek-KAY	therefore, so

Word Elision (Elisione)

Letters in between words will often be dropped to facilitate smooth pronunciation. This is a language phenomenon known as elision. When a word that ends in a vowel is followed by a word that starts with a vowel, the final vowel of the first word is often dropped and replaced with an apostrophe. In such cases, the vowel pronunciation and the stress are unchanged.

Examples:

the beloved	la amorosa> l'amorosa
the friend	lo amico > l'amico
where is	dove è > dov'è
the automobile	la automobile>l'automobile
this air	quelle aria> quell'aria
a university	una università > un'università
of Italy	di Italia>d'Italia
all is quiet	tutto è silenzio > tutt'è silenzio
it will be good	Sarà al buono > sar'al buono

The apostrophe may be omitted when masculine nouns and infinitives end with an "e". Hence:

| To make love | fare l'amore > far l'amore |
| Dr. Nardi | dottore Nardi > dottor Nardi |

Chapter 3: Common Italian Phrases

Now that you have a good grasp of Italian pronunciation, it's time to learn common greetings and useful phrases to make daily conversations a breeze. Following are key phrases you can use for different occasions:

Greetings/Common expressions:

Buongiorno!	Hello! / Good morning! (formal)
Ciao!	Hello!/Good-bye! (informal)
Salve!	Hello! / Good-bye! (neutral)
Arrivederci! (ah-ree-vuh-dehr-chee)	Goodbye! (formal)
Ciao!	Hello!/Good-bye! (informal)
Buonpomeriggio!	Good afternoon!
Buonasera!	Good afternoon!/Good evening! (formal)
Buonanotte!	Good night! (informal)
Come stai?	How are you?
Bene, grazie.	Fine, thank you.
Molto bene.	Very well.
Buona giornata!	Have a nice day!
Stai (stia) attento!	Take care!
A presto.	See you later.
Si.	Yes.
No.	No.
Per favore.	Please.
Mi scusi.	Excuse me.
Mi dispiace.	I'm sorry.
Non capisco.	I don't understand.
Meraviglioso!	Wonderful!

Aspetta!	Wait!
Torno subito.	I'll be right back.
Ripeti, per favore.	Please repeat.
Quanti anni hai?	How old are you?
Ci sentiamo dopo.	I'll talk to you later.
Buon compleanno!	Happy Birthday!
Congratulazioni!	Congratulations!
Buon Natale!	Merry Christmas!
Felice Anno Nuovo!	Happy New Year!
Buona Pasqua!	Happy Easter!
Buone vacanze!	Have a good holiday!
Buon viaggio!	Have a safe journey!
Buona fortuna!	Good luck!
Buon appetito!	Enjoy the meal!
Ovviamente.	Of course.
Questo dipende	That depends
Io non lo so	I don't know
Io penso di sì.	I think so.
Io non penso.	I don't think so.
Io suppongo di sì.	I suppose so.
Mi è indifferente.	I don't mind.
Non importa.	It doesn't matter.
Con piacere	wth pleasure
É vero	True
Chi?	Who?
Che cosa?	What?
Quando?	When?
Dove?	Where?
Perchè?	Why?
Quale?	Which?
Come?	How?
Quanto?	How Much?

Quanti?	How Many?

Introductions

To introduce yourself:

Mi chiamo (say your name).	My name is (your name).
Sono _____.	I'm (your name).

To introduce someone:

Ti presento il mio amico (name).	This is my (male) friend _____.
Ti presento la mia amica (name).	This is my (female friend _____.

To ask for the other person's name:

Lei come si chiama? (formal)	What is your name?
Come ti chiami? (familiar)	What is your name?

After the introductions, it's usual to express pleasure and appreciation.

1Pleased to meet you!	Piacere di conoscerla!
Nice to meet you!	Piacere!

Take note that the singular pronoun "you" in Italian has distinct forms for the formal and informal speech. The formal form, "Lei", is used to address a boss or a superior, older people, and new acquaintances. The informal form "tu" and "voi", its plural from, are used in conversations with family, friends, and younger people.

Here are other common exchanges:

Come sta? (formal)	How are you?
Come stai? (familiar)	How are you?
Come va?	How are things going?
Bene, grazie.	Fine, thank you.
Io sto bene, grazie.	I'm good, thank you.
Di dov'è Lei? (formal)	Where are you from?
Di dove sei? (familiar)	Where are you from?
Dove abiti? (singular)	Where do you live?
Dove abitate? (singular)	Where do you live?

Describing Yourself

Mi chiamo (your name) .	My name is _____.
Vengo da (country or place of origin) .	I'm from _____.
Ho (age in years) anni.	I'm _____ years old.
Il mio compleanno è il (day/month/year).	My birthday is _____.
Ho (number) fratelli e sorelle.	I have ____ siblings.
No, non ho fratelli e sorelle.	I have no siblings.
Ho (number) figli.	I have __ children.
Sono sposato/ sposata.	I'm married.
Non sono sposato/sposata.	I'm not married.
Il mio indirizzo è (your address) .	My address is _____.
Il mio numero di cellulare è (number) .	My cellphone number is ____.
Il mio posta elettonica è (e-mail address).	My e-mail address is _____.

Booking a Hotel Room

Quanto costa la camera?	How much is it for the room?
Vorrei una camera con ____.	I would like a room with ____.
letto matrimonial	a double bed
bagno private	private bathroom
l'aria condizionata	air conditioning
terrazza	terrace
il frigorifero	refrigerator
la televisione	television
on angolo cottura	with kitchenette
il telefono	telephone
l'acqua calda	hot water
bagno condiviso	shared bathroom

Hotel terms:

la cassaforte	safe deposit box
servizio sveglia	wake-up call
la chiave	key
l'ascensore	elevator
il riscaldamento	heat
il telecomando	remote control
il fax	fax
la sveglia	alarm clock
il portacenere	ash tray
le lenzuola	sheets
la coperta	blanket
l'asciugacapelli / il fon	blowdryer
il guardaroba	closet
la gruccia / la stampella	hanger
l'acqua minerale	mineral water
il ghiaccio	ice
il cuscino	pillow

lo shampoo	shampoo
il sapone	soap
la toilette	toilet
la carta igienica	toilet paper
l'asciugamano	towel

Ordering Food in a Restaurant

Waiter: -> Cosa prende? -> (What would you like?)

Phrases you can use:

Vorrei _____. (I would like _____.)
Vorrei ordinare _____.
(I would like to order _____.)

the colazione	breakfast
the pranzo	lunch
cena	dinner

Drinks:

acqua	water
l'acqua natural	still water
l'acqua leggermente gassata	slightly sparking water
l'acqua gassata	sparkling water
il succo	juice
vino	wine
il vino rosso	red wine
il vino bianco	white wine
il vino rosé	rose wine
birra	beer
caffè	coffee
caffè latte	coffee with milk.

latte	milk
tè	tea
un tazza di caffè	a cup of coffee
Una tazza di tè	a cup of tea
una bottiglia di vino	a bottle of wine
un bicchiere di acqua	a glass of water

Meat:

Agnello	lamb
maiale	pork
pollo	chicken
vitello	veal
manzo	beef
polpette	meatballs
scaloppini	escalope
coniglio	rabbit
trippa	tripe
la cotoletta	cutlet

Seafood:

i gamberi	prawns
l'aragosta	lobster
i calamari	squid
il granchio	crab
pesce	fish
le cozze	mussels
il baccalà	dried cod
il pesce spada	swordfish
la spigola	sea bass
il polpo	octopus

Miscellaneous food items:

riso	rice
antipasti	appetizers
cioccolata	chocolate
formaggio	cheese
fragola	strawberry
frutta	fruit
gelato	ice cream
insalata	salad
pane	bread
verdura	vegetables

Side dishes:

insalata	salad
insalata fresca	fresh salad
insalata di pollo	chicken salad
insalata mista	mixed salad
patate in insalata	potato salad

Condiments:

sale	salt
formaggio	cheese
pepe	pepper
sucherro	sugar
olio	oil
olio di semi	vegetable oil
olio d'oliva	olive oil
aceto balsamico	balsamic vinegar
aceto	vinegar

After the meal:

Il conto, per favore. – (The bill, please.)

Restaurant Vocabulary:

la scodella	the bowl
il tovagliolo	the napkin
il tavolo	the table
la sedia	the chair
il conto	the check
la caraffa	the pitcher
la tazza	the cup
il piatto	the plate
la forchetta	the fork
il coltello	the knife
il cucchiaio	the spoon
il cameriere	the waiter
la cameriera	the waitress
il menu	the menu
la mancia	the tip

Shopping

Italy is a great place for shopping and Italians are appreciated all over the world for their great sense of style. Here are important phrases you can use when shopping in Italian-speaking countries.

What the sales assistant usually say:

Posso aiutarla?	May I help you?
Cerca qualcosa?	What would you like?
Eccola.	Here it is.
Ha bisogno di altro?	Is that all?
Firmi qui per favore.	Please sign here.

Phrases you can use:

Quanto costa?	How much is this?
Vorrei _____.	I'd like _____.
Sto cercando _____.	I'm looking for _____.
Avete _____?	Do you have _____?
Posso provarla?	Can I try it on?
Lo prendo.	I'll take it.
Li prendo.	I'll take them all.
E' troppo caro.	It's too expensive.
Che misura e'?	What size is it?

Clothing sizes:

ho la taglia _____	I wear size ____
piccolo	small
medio	medium
grande	big, large
stretto	tight

largo	wide
corto	short
lungo	long
il numero di scarpa	shoe size

A department store (grandi magazzino) or street markets (mercato) will usually have a variety of stuff for shoppers. To look for specialty shops, you will find the following terms useful:

il negozio	the store
alimentary	grocery store
il supermercato	supermarket
la pasticceria	the pastry shop
la libreria	book store
la ferramenta	hardware store
il negozio di abbigliamento	clothes shop
la farmacia	the pharmacy
la profumeria	perfume shop
la gioielleria	jewelry shop
il negozio di giocattoli	toy shop
il negozio di articoli sportive	sports shop
La macelleria	butcher's shop
l'ottico	the optical shop
Il negozio di scarpe	shoe shop

Useful Shopping Terms:

l'entrata	entrance
l'uscita	exit
orario di aperture	opening hours
soldi	money
la cassa	cash desk
offerta special	son special offer

i saldi	sale (bargains)
aperto	open
chiuso	closed
borsa	bag
la carta de credito	credit card

Asking for Directions

Asking for and comprehending directions are important if you are in an unfamiliar place. Here are phrases you can use to ask for information.

Mi scusi, dov'è_____ ?	Excuse me, where is_____?
Come si arriva a____ ?	How do I get to____?
Potresti aiutarmi?	Can you help me?
Dov'è l'autobus?	Where is the bus?
Dove sono i tassì?	Where are the taxis?
Dov'è l'uscita?	Where is the exit?
Dove si troval la stazione?	Where is the train station?
E' qui vicino?	Is it near here?
Mi potrebbe portare a _____?	Could you take me to _____?

Important terms and phrases:

Va sempre diritto.	Just go straight.
giri a destroy	turn right
giri a sinistra	turn left
a sinistra	on the left
a destra	on the right
Si va indietro	Go back
accanto a	next to
verso	towards

Attraversa /Attraversi _____	Cross _____
Segua/ Segui _____	Follow _____
Vada/Vai_____	Go _____
una cartina	map
davanti a	in front of
di qua	over here
di fianco a	adjacent to
all'angolo	at the corner of
piazza	square
viale	avenue
città	city, town
strada	street, road
entrata	entrance
nord	north
sud	south
ovest	west
est	east
l'autostrada	motorway
semaforo	traffic lights
la rotatoria	roundabout
l'angolo	corner
di fronte	opposite
vicino a	close to, near
dietro	behind
prima	before
dopo	after
verso il basso	down
verso in giù	downwards
verso l'alto	up
verso in su	upwards
E' molto vicino.	It is very near.

E' piuttosto lontano.	It is quite far.
stazione	station
aeroporto	airport
indirizzo	address
in macchina	by car
a piedi	by foot

Common destinations:

il parco	the park
il centro storico	the historic center
il centro commercial	the shopping center
la stazione di polizia	the police station
l'agenzia di viaggio	the travel agency
il centro città	the town center
il ristorante	the restaurant
il monument	the monument
i bagni pubblici	the public restrooms
l'ospedale	the hospital
il municipio	the town hall
la periferia	the suburb
il bar	the bar
il museo	the museum

Transportation

When navigating around different places in Italy, you'll need to know important Italian phrases to take a taxi, ride a train, bus, or plane.

Taxi:

Dove posso noleggiare un taxi?	Where can I hire a taxi?
Mi porti a (destination), per favore.	Take me to _____, please.
Avanti.	Go straight on.
Segua la strada.	Follow the street.
Quanto costa la tariffa?	How much is the fare?

Taxi Vocabulary:

il tassista	taxi driver
il tassametro	taxi meter
il posteggio di taxi	taxi rank
la tariffa fissa	fixed fare
la tariffa	fare
la tariffa diurnal	day fare
la tariffa notturna	night fare
il cofano	car boot

Train:

Ho bisogno di un biglietto di sola andata per (destination) per favore.	I need a single ticket for (destination) please.
Mi dia un biglietto di ritorno per (destination), per favore.	Please give me a return ticket for (destination) .
Quando arriva lì?	When does it arrive here?
Devo cambiare?	Do I have to change?
Quanto dura il viaggio?	How long is the journey?

By Bus

Useful Phrases:

Dove si trova la stazione degli autobus?	Where is the bus station?
Ci sono posti liberi?	Are there vacant seats?
Questo posto è occupato.	This seat is taken.
Dove è il bus diretto a roma?	Where is the bus bound for Rome?
Quanto costa il biglietto a (destination) ?	How much is the fare to (destination)?
Quando è l' ultimo viaggio?	When is the last trip?

Transportation Vocabulary:

il viaggio	journey
il bagaglio	luggage
un blocchetto di biglietti	book of tickets
il guidatore dell'autobus	bus driver
la linea	line
il biglietto	Ticket
l'ufficio informazioni	information office
il viaggiatore	traveller
l'orario	timetable
il binario	platform
la partenza	departure
cambiare	to change
l'ufficio prenotazioni	booking office
la seconda classe	second class
non-fumatori	non-smoking
il posto	seat
scendere	to get off

Chapter 4: Italian Numbers

Cardinal Numbers

Italian numbers are written like most other European languages. A period is used instead of a comma while a comma is used in place of a period. Hence, one hundred twenty five thousand three hundred fifty and 30/100 will be written as 125.350,30. In addition, most numbers are written in one word.

1	One	Uno	OO-noh
2	Two	Due	DOO-eh
3	Three	Tre	TREH
4	Four	Quattro	KWAHT-troh
5	Five	Cinque	CHEEN-kweh
6	Six	Sei	SEH-ee
7	Seven	Sette	SET-the
8	Eight	Otto	OHT-toh
9	Nine	Nove	NOH-veh
10	Ten	Dieci	dee-EH-chee
11	Eleven	Undici	OON-dee-chee
12	Twelve	Dodici	DOH-dee-chee
13	Thirteen	Tredici	TREH-dee-chee
14	Fourteen	Quattordici	kwaht-TOR-dee-chee
15	Fifteen	Quindici	KWEEN-dee-chee
16	Sixteen	Sedici	SEH-dee-chee
17	Seventeen	Diciassette	dee-chahs-

			SET-teh
18	Eighteen	diciotto	dee-CHOHT-toh
19	Nineteen	diciannove	dee-chahn-NOH-veh
20	Twenty	venti	VEN-tee
21	twenty-one	ventuno	ven-TOO-noh
22	twenty-two	ventidue	ven-tee-DOO-eh
23	twenty-three	ventitré	ven-tee-TREH
24	twenty-four	ventiquattro	ven-tee-KWAHT-troh
25	twenty-five	venticinque	ven-tee-CHEEN-kweh
26	twenty-six	ventisei	ven-tee-SEH-ee
27	twenty-seven	ventisette	ven-tee-SET-the
28	twenty-eight	ventotto	ven-TOHT-toh
29	twenty-nine	ventinove	ven-tee-NOH-veh
30	thirty	trenta	TREN-tah
40	forty	quaranta	kwah-RAHN-tah
50	fifty	cinquanta	cheen-KWAHN-tah
60	sixty	sessanta	ses-SAHN-tah
70	seventy	settanta	set-TAHN-ta
80	eighty	ottanta	oht-TAHN-ta
90	ninety	Novanta	noh-VAHN-tah
100	one hundred	cento	CHEN-toh

101	one hundred one	centouno/ centuno	cheh-toh-OO-noh/chehn-TOO-noh
150	one hundred fifty	centocinquanta	cheh-toh-cheen-KWAHN-tah
200	two hundred	duecento	doo-eh-CHEN-toh
300	three hundred	trecento	treh-CHEN-toh
400	four hundred	quattrocento	kwaht-troh-CHEN-toh
500	five hundred	cinquecento	cheen-kweh-CHEN-toh
600	six hundred	Seicento	seh-ee-CHEN-toh
700	seven hundred	Settecento	set-the-CHEN-toh
800	eight hundred	Ottocento	oht-toh-CHEN-toh
900	nine hundred	Novecento	noh-veh-CHEN-toh
1.000	one thousand	Mille	MEEL-leh
1.001	one thousand one	Milleuno	meel-leh-OO-noh
1.200	one thousand two hundred	Milleduecento	meel-leh-doo-eh-CHEN-toh
2.000	two thousand	Duemila	doo-eh-MEE-lah
10.000	ten thousand	Diecimila	dee-eh-chee-MEE-lah
15.000	fifteen thousand	Quindicimila	kween-dee-chee-MEE-lah
100.000	one hundred	Centomila	chen-toh-mee-leh

	thousand		
1.000.000	one million	un milione	OON mee-lee-OH-neh
2.000.000	two million	due milioni	DOO-eh mee-lee-OH-neh
1.000 .000.000	one billion	un miliardo	OON mee-lee-ARE-doh

Ordinal Numbers

1st	primo
2nd	secondo
3rd	terzo
4th	quarto
5th	quinto
6th	sesto
7th	settimo
8th	ottavo
9th	nono
10th	decimo
11th	undicesimo
12th	dodicesimo
14th	tredicesimo
14th	quattordicesimo
15th	quindicesimo
16th	sedicesimo
17th	diciassettesimo
18th	diciottesimo
19th	diciannovesimo
20th	ventesimo
21st	ventunesimo
22nd	ventiduesimo

23rd	ventitreesimo
24th	ventiquattresimo
25th	venticinquesimo
26th	ventiseiesimo
27th	ventisettesimo
28th	ventottesimo
29th	ventinovesimo
30th	trentesimo
40th	quarantesimo
50th	cinquantesimo
60th	sessantesimo
70th	settantesimo
80th	ottantesimo
90th	novantesimo
100th	centesimo
200th	duecentesimo
300th	trecentesimo
400th	quattrocentesimo
500th	cinquecentesimo
600th	seicentesimo
700th	settecentesimo
800th	ottocentesimo
900th	novecentesimo
1,000th	millesimo
10,000th	diecimillesimo
100,000th	centomillesimo
1,000,000th	millionesimo
1,000,000,00th	milliardesimo

Chapter 5: Months and Days

When making travel arrangements, you need to know how to express the date properly to avoid confusion or missed flights and opportunities.

It's important to know that when writing dates, Italian begins with the day before the month and the year. For example, to express November 30, 2015, you should write 30/11/15.

In Italian, the months and days do not begin with a capital letter.

Months of the Year (I giorni della settimana)

gennaio	January
febbraio	February
marzo	March
aprile	April
maggio	May
giugno	June
luglio	July
agosto	August
settembre	September
ottobre	October
novembre	November
dicembre	December

Days of the Week i (Giorni della settimana)

lunedì	Monday
martedì	Tuesday
mercoledì	Wednesday
giovedì	Thursday

venerdì	Friday
sabato	Saturday
domenica	Sunday

The Seasons (Le Stagioni)

Spring	spring	March to May
Summer	estate	June to August
Autumn	autunno	September to November
Winter	inverno	December to February

Chapter 6: Telling Time, Dates, Year, and Century

Italians generally use the 24-hour clock which is just a matter of adding 12 to the hours after noon. For instance, if the clock says 3 in the afternoon, it's written as 15:00.

To ask for the specific time, you can use the following expressions:

What time is it?	"Che ore sono?" or "Che ora è?"
What time do you have?	"Che hora fai?"

To tell the time, you will use a definite article in the feminine form before the specific time. The singular linking verb "è" (is) is used to tell time when the hour is at 1 o'clock. The plural verb "sono" (are) is used to express time for all other hours. To express time between the hours, you'll simply tell the hour and the minutes separating both time elements with the word "e" which means "and".

Examples:

It's 3:21 AM.	Sono le tre e ventuno.
It's 1:15 AM.	É l'una e un quarto.
It's 5:23 PM.	Sono le diciassette e ventitrè.
It's 9:30 AM.	Sono le nove e mezzo.
It's 4:25 PM.	Sono le sedici e venticinque.
It's noon.	É mezzogiorno.
It's midnight.	É mezzanotte.

When the minutes are past the half hour, you will use "meno" which means less and state the minutes before the approaching hour.

Example:

It's quarter to four AM.	Sono le quattro meno un quarto.
It's ten minutes to six PM.	Sono le diciotto meno dieci.
It's twenty five minutes to 9 AM.	So le nove meno venticinque.

Useful Time Expressions:

ieri	yesterday
domain	tomorrow
oggi	today
now	adesso
una settimana fa	a week ago
l'altro ieri	the other day
dopodomani	the day after tomorrow
di qui a un mese	a month from now
tra una settimana	in a week
a volte	sometimes
ogni due settimane	every two weeks
ogni giorno	every day
la settimana prossima	next week
la settimana scorsa	last week
a metà ottobre	in the middle of October
ogni tanto	from time to time
affitto di un mese	rental for one month

Italians use this order to express the date: day/month/year. Hence, to express December 5, 2015, you will write 5/12/2015.

Expressing Year and Century

To state the year, just write the thousands, hundreds, tens, and the unit.

For example:

2015	duemilaquindici
2014	duemilaquattordici
1942	millenovecentoquarantadue

To express the century, Italians use the word "secolo"

For example:

In the 20th century	nel ventesimo secolo
In the 21st century	nel ventunesima secolo
in the 19th century	nel diciannovesimo secolo

Useful Expressions:

fra il 2004 ed il 2015	between 2004 and 2015
dal agosto 2015	as of August 2015
Ho lavorato fino al 2014.	I worked until 2014.
Nel luglio 2014	in July 2014
nell'anno tre	in year 3

Chapter 7: Colors in Italian

Colors are used to describe people and things around us. In Italian, most colors are declined to agree with the gender and number of the word being described.

Examples:

un cane nero	a black dog
una macchina gialla	a yellow car
quattro cani neri	four black dogs
3 case bianche	three white houses

Here are the most common color words:

rosso	red
blu	blue
giallo	yellow
arancione	orange
nero	black
verde	green
bianco	white
rosso Bordeaux	maroon
biondo	blonde
rosa	pink
marrone	brown
viola	purple
castano	brunette
grigio	gray
violetto	violet
blu chiaro	light blue

oro	gold
argento	silver

Chapter 8: Forming Sentences

The basic Italian sentence structure is similar to that of English:

Subject + Verb + Object

Hence:

<u>Janina</u> <u>parla</u> <u>francese</u>.

Subject+Verb+Object

There are a few differences between English and Italian clause and sentence structure.

In English, adjectives come before the noun they describe – the pink dress, the intelligent girls, and the blue car. In Italian, with a few exceptions, adjectives usually come after the word they describe – il vestito rosa, le ragazze intelligente, le auto blu.

Italian sentences need not follow the standard Subject+Verb+Object word order. To change the emphasis of a sentence, the verb can come before the subject.

Annie arriverà domain.	Annie will arrive tomorrow.
Arriverà Annie domain.	Annie will arrive tomorrow.

In Italian, the subject pronoun is usually omitted because it is clearly indicated by the verb form.

Italian Negation

The most common away to express negation in Italian is by using the word "non" before the verb. In some cases, the object pronoun may come before the verb.

For example:

Sono felice.	I am happy.
Io non sono felice.	I am not happy.

Gli piace il cibo.	He likes the food.
Non gli piace il cibo.	He doesn't like the food.

Here are other **negative expressions** in Italian:

Io non guido	I don't drive
non guida	he doesn't drive
Non guidiamo	we don't drive
non do	I don't give
non dà	he doesn't give
non diamo	we don't give
Non amo	I don't love
egli non ama	he doesn't love

non amiamo	we don't love
non sorridere	I don't smile
egli non sorride	he doesn't smile
non sorridiamo	we don't smile
Non parlo	I don't speak
non parla	he doesn't speak
non parliamo	we don't speak
Non prendo	I don't take
egli non prende	he doesn't take
noi non prendiamo	we don't take
Io non scrivo	I don't write
egli non scrive	he doesn't write
non scriviamo	we don't write

Chapter 9: Capitalization and Punctuation

Capitalization

The Italian language has less use for the capital letter than English. The following words are capitalized in English but not in Italian:

months of the year and days of the week

gennaio, febbraio, marzo, lunedi, martedi, mercoledi

proper adjectives

un libro francese, la lingua spagnola

a few proper nouns

nouns of nationalities such as americani (Americans), francese (French)

titles like Mr., Mrs., Ms., or Miss: Il signor Ramon è italiano. Mr. Ramon is Italian.

Useful terms:

carrateri minuscoli - lower case or small letters

carrateri maiuscoli - upper case or capital big letters

Punctuation

Here are the most commonly-used punctuation marks in Italian:

.	il punto	period
,	la virgola	comma
?	il punto interrogativo	question mark
!	il punto esclamativo	exclamation point
:	due punti	colon
;	il punto e virgola	semicolon
'	l'apostrofo	apostrophe

—	la lineetta	dashes
-	il trattino	hyphen
...	i puntini di sospensione	ellipses
*	l'asterisco	asterisk
« »	le virgolette	quotation marks
[]	le parentesi quadre	brackets
()	le parentesi tonde	brackets

Chapter 10: Nouns (Nomi)

Nouns are words that name people, places, animal, things, or ideas. Italian nouns take on different forms to indicate their number and gender. The articles, adjectives, and other modifiers must agree with the number and gender of the noun being described or modified. A noun can be used as a subject, object of a verb, or an object of a preposition.

Gender

Italian nouns can only take one of two genders – the masculine or feminine gender. When learning the gender of nouns, it is best to learn the noun along with the definite article that comes with the noun.

The grammatical gender of a noun generally follows the natural gender of the person being referred to. Hence, female human beings are feminine while male human beings are masculine. Collective nouns with mixed genders are masculine.

Masculine nouns:

Il padre	the father
il figlio	the son
lo zio	the uncle
maestro	male teacher
bambini	children (all boys)

Feminine nouns:

la madre	the mother
la figlia	the daughter
la zia	the aunt
bambine	children (all girls)

Collective Nouns with mixed genders

bambini	children (boys and girls)

For animals, things, places, and ideas, there are basic guidelines to identify the gender of the noun. One way is by checking the ending. Here are guidelines you can apply:

In general, most Italian nouns with –o ending are masculine.

il libro	the book
il museo	the museum
il corpo	the body
il tavolo	the table
il cielo	the sky
il suono	the sound

The exceptions to this rule include the following nouns:

la mano	the hand
la radio	the radio
la biro	the pen

Another group of exception includes feminine nouns that only happened to end in –o because of the shortening done on the word.

l'auto (short form for l'automobile)	the car
la foto (short form for la fotografia)	the picture
la moto (short form for la motocicletta)	the motorbike

Most nouns ending in –a are feminine

la finestra	the window
la città	the city
la sedia	the chair
la pizza	the pizza
la penna	pen

Exceptions:

Nouns ending in –ma are masculine:

il cinema	the cinema
il tema	the theme
il fantasma	the ghost
il panorama	the panorama
il problema	the problem
il programa	the program
il clima	the climate

A few proper nouns that end in –a are masculine, including the name "Andrea".

Nouns ending in –a which are of Greek origin and nouns ending in –cida and –ista can be masculine or feminine depending on the context in which they are used.

il colega	collegue
atleta	athlete
suicida	suicide
turista	tourist
giornalista	journalist
pianist	pianist
artista	artist

In general, nouns ending in –e are either masculine or feminine:

la nave	the ship
la luce	the light
la mente	the mind
il dente	the tooth
la nube	the cloud
il bicchiere	the glass

As you can expect, there are exceptions to the rule:

Nouns that end in –ie are feminine.

la specie	the kind
La superficie	the surface

All nouns that end in –ore are masculine.

il fattore	the farmer
il motore	the engine
il colore	the color
il autore	author

Nearly all nouns ending in –ite, –udine, -ice, -ione, and –igine are feminine.

la lite	the quarrel
la altitudine	the height
la pittrice	the painter
la decisione	the decision
la visione	the vision
la nazione	the nation
l'origine	the origin

A majority of nouns ending in –ame, –ale, -ere, and -ile are masculine.

Il rame	the copper
il giornale	the newspaper
Il pollame	the poultry
il canale	the channel
Il potere	the power
il canile	the kennel

Nouns ending in -tù and -tà are all feminine.

la servitú	the slavedom
la gioventù	the youth
la gioventù	the youth
la virtú	the virtue
la felicità	the happiness

In general, nouns ending in -i are feminine.

l'analisi	the analysis
la sintesi	the synthesis
la crisi	the crisis

The exception includes nouns like il safari (safari) and il brindisi (toast).

Italian nouns with a consonant ending are mostly of foreign origin and are generally masculine.

il computer	the computer
lo sport	the sport
il bar	the bar
il toast	the toast
il film	the film

Exceptions include nouns like la holding (holding) and la star (star).

In some cases, noun genders may be established by what the word denotes.

Seas and lakes are grammatically masculine.

il Pacifico	the Pacific
il Tirreno	the Tyrrhenian

Branches of science are feminine nouns.

la chimica	the chemistry
la biologia	the biology

Cities are feminine.

la Città di Londra	the City of London

Names of chemical elements and metals are masculine.

il bronzo	the bronze
il cesio	cesium
l'alluminio	the aluminum
l'oro	gold
l'argento	silver

Names of trees are generally masculine.

il pero	the pear tree
l'acero	the maple tree
Il melo	the apple tree
l'albero di mogano	the mahogany tree
Il ciliegio	the cherry tre

Some trees, however, have feminine gender:

la palma	the palm tree
la quercia	the oak tree
la vite	the grapevine

Forming Feminine Nouns

In general, an Italian noun is expressed and listed in a masculine form. In many cases, a masculine noun's ending is changed to form the feminine. In some instances, feminine words would have completely different form from the masculine.

Changing the Ending to Form the Feminine Nouns

Masculine Nouns ending in -o

To form the feminine, the −o ending is replaced with an −a ending:

Examples:

il gatto	male cat	la gatta	female cat
il bambino	little boy	la bambina	little girl
il figlio	son	la figlia	daughter
il zio	uncle	la zia	aunt

Masculine Nouns ending in −a

To form the feminine, the -a ending is replaced with an −essa ending:

il duca	duke	la duchessa	duchess
il poeta	male poet	la poetessa	female poet

Masculine nouns ending in −e

To form the feminine, the −e ending is either replaced with −a or dropped and replaced with −essa:

il padrone	master	la padrona	house mistress
il signore	mister	la signora	mistress
il principe	prince	la principessa	the princess

Masculine nouns ending in −tore

A majority of nouns that end with −tore form the feminine by replacing the ending with −trice. Several nouns with −tore ending form take the suffix −tora.

il direttore	director	la direttrice	the directress
il pattore	male painter	la pittrice	female painter
Il pastore	shepherd	la pastora	shepherdress

Nouns with Totally Distinct Forms for Masculine and Feminine

Some nouns are derived from completely different roots and differ completely in the masculine and feminine form:

il uomo	man	la donna	woman
il fratello	brother	la sorella	sister
il padre	father	la madre	mother
il padrino	godfather	la madrina	godmother
il frate	friar	la suora	nun
el re	king	la regina	queen
il maschio	male	la femmina	female
il marito	husband	la moglie	wife
il cane	dog	la cagna	bitch

The Epicene Gender

Several nouns have one form for both genders. To indicate the gender, the words "maschio"and "femmina" are used to modify the masculine and feminine gender respectively.

la cicogna maschio	the male stork
la cicogna femmina	the female stork
l'acquila maschio	the male eagle
l'acquila femmina	the female eagle
la volpe mascchio	the male fox
la volpe femmina	the female fox
il serpent maschio	the male snake
la serpent femmina	the female snake

Forming Plural Nouns

In general, Italian nouns form the plural by changing the ending of its singular form.

Nouns ending in −a

Masculine nouns ending in −a form the plural by changing the ending to −i while feminine nouns form the plural by changing the ending to −e.

Examples:

Masculine nouns ending in -a

Singular	Plural	English
l'artista	gli artisti	the artist, the artists
il poeta	i poeti	the poet, the poets
il proglema	i problemi	the problem, the problems

Feminine nouns ending in -a

Singular	Plural	English
la cosa	le cose	the thing, the things
la casa	le case	the house, the houses
la porta	le porte	the door, the doors
l'agenzia	le agenize	the agency, the agencies

Nouns ending in -o

Nouns that end in –o form their plural by changing the ending to –i for both genders.

Masculine nouns ending in -o

Singular	Plural	English
il libro	i libri	the book, the books
il bambino	i bambini	the male child, the children
il giorno	i giorni	the day, the days
il amico	I amici	the male friend, the male friends

Feminine nouns ending in -o

Singular	Plural	English
la mano	le mani	the hand, the hands

Nouns ending in –e

Nouns that end in –e form the plural by changing the ending to –i for both genders.

Masculine nouns ending in –e

Singular	Plural	English
il dente	i denti	the tooth, the teeth
il bicchiere	i bicchiere	the glass, the glasses
il cane	i cani	the dog, the dogss
il padre	i padre	the father, the fathers

Feminine nouns ending in –e

la luce	le luci	the light, the lights
la canzone	le canzoni	the song, the songs
la madre	le madri	the mother, the mothers

Nouns with different endings form their plural in different ways.

Nouns ending in –ca

Masculine nouns ending –ca form the plural by changing its ending to –chi while feminine nouns that end in –ca form their plural by changing the ending to –che.

Examples:

Masculine nouns ending in -ca

il monarca	i monarchi	the monarch, the monarchs
il patriarca	i patriarchi	the patriarch, the patriarchs
il duca	i duchi	the duke, the dukes

Feminine nouns ending in –ca

la amica	le amiche	female friend, female friends
la mucca	le mucche	the cow, the cows
la barca	le barche	the boat, the boats
la basilica	le basiliche	the church, the churches

Nouns ending in −ga

Masculine nouns that end in −ga form the plural by changing the ending to −ghi while feminine nouns that end in −ga form the plural by changing the ending to −ghe.

Examples:

Masculine nouns ending in -ga

il collega	i colleghi	the colleague, the colleagues
lo stratega	gli streteghi	the strategy, the strategies

Feminine nouns ending in -ga

la strega	le streghe	the witch, the witches
la bottega	le botteghe	the store, the stores

Nouns ending in −gia and −cia form the plural in different ways

Nouns with stressed or tonic "i" in −gia or −cia form the plural by dropping the −a and changing the noun's ending to −gie and −cie respectively.

la bugìa	le bugìe	the lie, the lies
la farmacìa	le farmacìe	the pharmacy, the pharmacies

Nouns with unstressed or atonic "i" form the plural by maintaining the "i" if –gia or –cia are immediately preceded by a vowel. The 'i" is dropped if –gia and –cia are immediately preceded by a consonant.

Examples:

la valìgia	le valigie	the suitcase, the suitcases
l'arancia	le arance	the orange, the oranges
la ciliegia	le ciliegie	the cherry, the cherries

Nouns ending in –io

The following rules govern the plural formation of nouns that end in –io:

If the "i" is stressed or tonic, the plural is formed by changing the ending to –ii

Singular	Plural	
il rinvio	i rinvìi	the postponement, the postponements
il zio	i zii	the uncle, the uncles

If "i" is unstressed or atonic, the noun's ending to is changed to –I to form the plural.

Singular	Plural	
Il figlio	i figli	the son, the sons
Ilcambio	i càmbii	the change, the changes

Nouns that Change its Gender When Forming the Plural

A few masculine nouns that end in –o become feminine in the plural form.

Singular	Plural	
il miglio	le miglia	the mile, the miles
il centinaio	le centinaia	the hundred, the hundreds
il riso	le risa	the laugh, the laughs
l'uovo	le uova	the egg, the eggs
il paio	le paia	the pair, the pairs

Nouns with Irregular Plural Forms

Some nouns change their stem to express the plural:

l'ala	le ali	the wing, the wings
il dio	gli dei	the god, the gods
il tempio	i temple	the temple, the temples
l'arma	le armi	the weapon, the weapons

Plural Formation of Nouns Ending in –co or -go

Italian nouns ending in –co and –go form their plural in several ways and must be learned individually.

In general, nouns ending in –co or –go change to plural in the following manner:

If the noun is stressed on the penultimate syllable, it forms the plural by changing –co to –chi and –go to –ghi. These nouns are called parole piane.

If the noun is stressed on the third syllable counting from the final one, it forms the plural by changing –co to –ci and –go to –gi. These words are called parole sdrucciole.

Examples:

Parole Piane

Singular	Plural
il fuòco (the fire)	i fuochi (the fires)
il albèrgo (the hotel)	i albergi (the hotels)

Notable exceptions:

il greco (the Greek)	i greci (the Greeks)
il porco (the pork)	i porci (the pigs)
il amico (the friend)	i amici (the friends)
il nemico (the enemy)	i nemici (the enemies)

Parole Sdrucciole

Singular	Plural
il sìndaco (the Mayor)	i sindaci (the Mayors)
l'aspàrago (the asparagus)	gli asparagi (the asparagus)

Notable exceptions:

il incarico (the assignment)	i incarichi (the assignments)
il valico (the crossing)	i valichi (the crossings)
l'abico (the abico)	gli abachi (the abici)
il strascico (the train)	i strascichi (the trains)
il carico (the load)	i carichi (the loads)
l'abaco (the abacus)	gli abachi (the abacuses)

Invariable Nouns

Many Italian nouns have the same form in singular and plural. These nouns are usually modified by a corresponding article to distinguish their number.

Nouns ending in -i

5lo àlibi	the alibi	gli alibi	the alibis
lo àlcali	the alkali	gli àlcali	the alkalis
la cisti	the cyst	le cisti	the cysts
la crisi	the crisis	le crisi	the crises
la analisi	the analysis	le analisi	the analyses
la paràlisi	the paralysis	le paralisi	the paralyses
la paràfrasi	the paraphrase	le parafrasi	the paraphrases
la ipotesi	the hypothesis	le ipotesi	the hypotheses
la parèntesi	the parenthesis	le parèntesi	the parentheses
la ipòfisi	the hypophysis	le ipofisi	the hypophyses
la tèsi	the dissertation	le tèsi	the dissertations
la paràbasi	the parabasis	le parabasi	the parabases

Monosyllabic nouns

il dì	the day	i dì	the days
il tè	the tea	i tè	the teas
il sì	the yes	i sì	the yeses
il re	the king	i re	the kings
il su	the up	i su	the ups

Nouns ending in an accented vowel:

la beltà	the beauty	le beltà	the beauties
il canapè	the sofa	I canapè	the sofas
il babà	the rum cake	i babà	the rum cakes
il caffè	the coffee	i caffè	the coffees
la civiltà	the civilization	le civiltà	the civilizations
il paltò	the overcoat	i paltò	the overcoats
il bebé	the baby	i bebé	the babies
il pascià	the pasha	i pascià	the pashas
la città	the city	le città	the cities
il papa	the father	i papa	the fathers
lo emù	the emu	gli emù	the emus
la virtù	the virtue	le virtù	the virtues
la università	the university	la università	the universities

In general, nouns derived from foreign terms:

il drive	the drive	i drive	the drives
il software	the software	i software	the software
il goal	the goal	i goal	the goals
il mouse	the mouse	i mouse	the mice
il panama	the Panama hat	i panama	the Panama hats
la mousse	the mousse	le mousse	the mousses
il film	the film	i film	the films
la paella	the paella	le paella	the paellas
il pâté	the pâté	i pâté	the pâtés
il pastiche	the pastiche	i pastiche	the pastiche
la performance	the performance	le performance	the performances
il party	the party	i party	the parties

Abbreviated nouns

automobile	la àuto	the car	le auto	the cars
paracadutista	il parà	the paratrooper	i parà	the paratroopers
motocicleta	la mòto	the bike	le mòto	the bikes
il radioricevitore	la ràdio	the radio	le radio	the radios
cinematografo	il cìnema	the movie theater	i cinema	movie theatres
stereofonico	lo stereo	the stereo	gli stereo	the stereos
la videocassette	il video	the videotape	i video	the videotapes

Nouns ending in a consonant

lo autobus	the bus	gli autobus	the buses
il monitor	the monitor	i monitor	the monitors
il bar	the café	i bar	the cafes
il pallet	the pallet	i pallet	the pallets
il computer	the computer	i computer	the computers
il pandit	the pundit	i pandit	the pundits
il condor	the condor	i condor	the condors
il parquet	the wood floor	i parquet	the wood floors
il modem	the modem	i modem	the modems
il tram	the cable car	i tram	the cable cars
il pancreas	the pancreas	i pancreas	the pancreases
lo scanner	the scanner	gli scanner	the scanners
il pantheon	the Pantheon	i pantheon	the Pantheons
il radar	the radar	i radar	the radars
lo sport	the sport	gli sport	the sports

Masculine neologism ending in –o

il Euro (the Euro)	i Euro (the Euros)

Some feminine nouns ending in –ie

la serie (the series)	le serie (the series)
l'especie (the species)	le especie (the species)

Defective Nouns (Nomi Difettivi)

Nouns that only take the singular form and those that only take the plural form are classified as defective nouns. The following are defective nouns:

Singularia Tantum (Nouns which appear mostly or exclusively in the singular form)

Nouns designating substances, metals, materials, chemical elements, and products

il latte	the milk
il bronzo	the bronze
l'ossigeno	the oxygen
il carbone	the coal
l'ottone	the brass
l'idrogeno	the hydrogen
il ferro	the iron
il frumento	the wheat
l'oro	the gold

Most abstract nouns denoting state, action, or quality

l'amore	the love

la pazienza	the joy
la gioia	the joy
il corragio	the courage
la pietà	the compassion
l'onore	the honor
l'intelligenza	the intelligence
la bellezza	the beauty
lo sviluppo	the development
l'ingratitudine	the ingratitude
l'orgoglio	the pride
il valore	the valor

Take note that a few abstract nouns can be expressed in the plural but will take on a different meaning. For instance, la belleza (the beauty) has a plural form, le bellezze, but it refers to either beautiful places or beautiful women.

Names of diseases

Il tifo	the typhus
il colera	the cholera
la malaria	the malaria
il morbillo	measles
il vaiolo	the smallpox
l'influenza	the flu
il morbillo	the measles
l'Aids	the AIDS

Nouns that denote unique objects or phenomena

il sole	the sun
il sud	the south
il nord	the north

l'orizzonte	the horizon
la luna	the moon

Names of months

gennaio	January
febbraio	February
marzo	March
aprile	April

Nouns referring to food and drinks

Il latte	milk
Il cioccolato	chocolate
l'orzo	barley
il pane	bread
il pepe	pepper
il riso	rice
il grano	wheat
il miele	honey

Nouns pertaining to the sciences and those ending in -ismo

la biologia	biology.
la chimica	chemistry
la medicina	medical science
l'impressionismo	impressionism

Some collective nouns

il fogliame	foliage
la gente	people
la roba	stuff

Proper Nouns

Germania	Germany
Roma	Rome
Carlota	Carlota
Stati Uniti	United States

Pluralia Tantum (Nouns which appear mostly or exclusively in the plural form)

Nouns referring to objects with two paired or similar components

i calzone	pants
le forbici	scissors
le tenàglie	tongs, pliers
le mutande	underwear
gli occhiali	glasses
gemèlli	twins
le narici	nostrils

Nouns which refer to a group of objects of similar type

le masserizie	housewares
lespèzie	spices
le vettovaglie	provisions
i dintorni	surroundings
le stoviglie	dishes

le macerie	ruins
le vettovàglie	viand
le tènebre	darkness

A few nouns derived from Latin

le ferie	holiday
le nozze	wedding

Nomi sovrabbondandi

Several Italian nouns have two singular forms, two plural forms, or two singular and plural forms.

Nouns with two singulars

Nouns with two singular end in –iero or –iere and are all masculine.

English	Common Form	Literary Form	
	Singular	Singular	Plural
steed	il destriero	il destriere	i destrieri
foreigner	il forestiero	il forestiere	i forestieri
sparrowhawk	lo sparviero	lo sparviere	gli sparvieri

Nouns with two plurals

Nouns with two plural forms can be grouped into two:

Nouns with plural forms that have dissimilar meanings

Nouns with plural forms that have similar meanings

Nouns that have two plural forms with dissimilar meanings:

Singular		Masculine Plural		Feminine Plural	
il bràccio	arm	i bracci	wings, branches	le bràccio	human arms
il muro	wall	i muri	building walls	le mura	city walls
il dito	finger	i diti	fingers, individual	le dita	fingers, collective
il como	horn	i como	horns/instrument	le coma	animal horns
il labbro	edge, lip	i labbri	edges	le labra	lips
lo anèllo	ring	gli anèlli	rings	le anèlla	curly hairs
lo òsso	bone	gli òssi	animal bones	le òssa	human bones
il ciglio	edge	i cigli	edges	le ciglia	eyelash
il grido	cry	i gridi	animal's cries	le grida	human's cries
il gesto	gesture	i gesti	gestures	le gesta	deeds

Nouns that have plural forms with similar meanings

There are only a few nouns in this category. Here are some of them:

Singular		Masculine Plural		Feminine Plural	
lo urlo	shout	gli urli	shouts	le urla	shouts
il ginòcchio	knee	i ginòcchi	knees	le ginòcchia	knees
il gomito	elbow	i gomiti	elbows	le gomita	elbows
lo stride	squeak	gli stridi	squeaks	le strida	squeaks
il filament	filament	i filaménti	filaments	le filaménta	filaments

Nouns with Two Singular Forms and Two Plural Forms

There are two Italian nouns with two singular forms and two plural forms. In addition, both forms have similar meaning.

Singular Forms		Plural Forms		English
l'orecchia	l'orecchio	le orecchie	gli orecchi	ear
la strofe	la strofa	le strofi	le strofe	strophe

Chapter 11: Articles (Gli Articoli)

The Italian language has two main types of articles, the definite articles and the indefinite articles. Unlike their English counterparts, Italian articles must agree with both gender and number of the nouns they modify. In addition, articles may change in form if the noun being modified starts with a vowel. Hence, the article forms vary according to the gender, number, and first letter of the word they modify.

Definite Articles (Articoli determinativi)

Definite articles modify nouns that refer to a particular person, things, place, or idea.

Gender	Singular	Plural
Masculine	il	i
Masculine	lo	gli
Feminine	la	le
Masculine/Feminine	l'	gli/le

The articles "il" and "i" are used to modify masculine nouns that start with a consonant except when the articles "lo" and "gli" must be used. The articles "lo" and "gli" are used to modify masculine nouns that start with z, x, gn, pn, ps, i, y+vowel, and s+consonant. In addition, "lo" changes to "l'" when the word that comes after it starts with an "h" or a vowel.

Examples:

Singular		Plural	
il telefono	the telephone	i telefoni	the telephones
il libro	the book	i libri	the books

il pollo	the chicken	i pollo	the chicken
lo specchio	the mirror	gli specchi	the mirrors
lo zucchero	the sugar	gli zucchero	the sugar
lo xilofono	the xylophone	gli xilofoni	the xylophones
		gli spaghetti	the spaghetti

The articles "la" and "le" are used before feminine nouns. For ease in pronunciation, the article "la" is contracted to " l' " if the following word starts with a vowel but no contraction is done for the feminine plural form of the article.

la sedia	the chair	le sedie	the chairs
la matita	the pencil	le matite	the pencils
la finestra	the window	le fnestre	the windows
la strada	the street	le strade	the streets
l'arancia	the orange	le arance	the oranges
l'amica	the girlfriend	le amiche	the girlfriends
l'entrata	the entrance	le entrate	the entrances
l'orologio	the watch	gli orologi	the watches

Chapter 12: Indefinite Articles (Articoli indeterminativi)

The indefinite article is equivalent to "a" or "an" in the English language and corresponds to the number "one'. They are used before nouns that are known but are not specifically identified. Indefinite articles have no plural forms and plural nouns that are not specifically identified can take the partitive article if needed.

5Gender	Indefinite Articles
Masculine	uno / un
Feminine	una / un

The indefinite article "uno" is used before a masculine singular noun that begins with S+consonant, z, x, y+vowel, gn, ps, or pn.

Examples:

uno stato	a state
uno schizzo	a sketch
uno psicologo	a psychologist
uno zio	an uncle
uno yacht	a yacht
uno pneumatico	a tire
uno stadio	a stage
uno specchio	a mirror
uno gnomo	a gnome
uno xilofono	a xylophone
uno zoccolo	a hoof

The indefinite article "un" is used before all other masculine singular noun that does not require the article "uno".

Examples:

un quaderno	a notebook
un libro	a book
un amico	friend
un piatto	a dish
un giornale	a newspaper
un orologio	a clock
un uomo	a man
un treno	a train
un albero	a tree
un ristorante	a restaurant
un aereo	a plane

The indefinite article "una" is used before feminine nouns that start with a consonant.

Examples:

una macchina	a car
una notte	a night
una casa	a house
una penna	a pen
una bicicletta	a bicycle
una biblioteca	a library
una sedia	a chair
una stazione	a station

The indefinite article "un" introduces feminine singular nouns that start with a vowel.

un' infermiera	a nurse
un'amica	a friend
un' insalata	a salad
un'automobile	a car
un'ora	an hour
un'ọpera	an opera
un'arancia	an orange

Partitive articles (Articoli partitivi)

Partitive articles are used to denote approximate or indefinite quantities. They correspond to the words "some" or "any" in English. The partitive article is formed by combining the "de" form of the preposition "di" (of with the appropriate definite article. The rules on the usage of definite articles apply to partitive articles.

Gender	Singular	Plural
masculine	del	dei
masculine	dello	degli
feminine	della	delle
masculine/ feminine	dell'	degli/delle

Examples:

del pane	some bread
delle arance	some oranges
dell'olio	some oil
del burro	some butter
degli spaghetti	some spaghetti
della gente	some people
dei panini	a few rolls
dello zucchero	any sugar
dell'acqua	some water

Chapter 13 Pronouns (Pronomi)

Personal pronouns replace persons or things in a sentence or phrase and can function as a subject or object.

Subject Pronouns (Pronomi soggetto

Subject pronouns are often omitted because the verb's conjugation already indicates the person. There are instances, however, that requires the use of subject pronouns: for clarity, to emphasize something, or when the adverb "anche" (also is used to modify the pronoun.

Subject Pronouns	English
io	I
tu	you
lui	he (familiar
lei	she
egli	he (written
noi	we
voi	you
loro	they
Loro	you (formal
esso (m	it
essa (f	it
essi (m, neuter	they
esse (f, neuter	they

Take note that when it comes to personal pronoun, Italian has distinct forms for the neuter gender. The neuter pronouns are used to replace animals and objects.

Examples:

Io pulisco la casa.	I clean the house.
Noi siamo tristi.	We are sad.
Loro sono in ritardo.	We are late.
Siete molto generoso.	You are very generous.
Lei sta bene.	She is fine.

Object Pronouns (Oggetto Pronomi

Object pronouns require a verb and are either direct or indirect. Pronouns used as a direct object receives the verb's action while those that are used as indirect objects are indirectly affected by the verb.

Direct object Pronouns (Pronomi Diretti

A direct object pronoun replaces a noun used as a direct object. Below are the Italian direct object pronouns:

Singular	
mi	me
ti	you
La (2nd person polite	you
lo	him, it
la	her, it
Plural	
ci	us
vi	you
li	them (male
le	them (female
Li (2nd person polite	them (male

86

Le (2nd person polite	them (female

The third person direct object pronouns in the singular form are frequently shortened as l'. The polite forms for the second person pronouns are capitalized.

Usage

Li <u>ho</u> visti alla festa.	I saw them at the party last night.
Abbiamo dato <u>loro</u> fiori.	We gave them flowers.

Indirect Object Pronouns

An indirect object pronoun answers the question for whom or to whom. Their forms are almost identical to direct object pronouns.

Singolare	Singular (to/for	Plurale	Plural (to/for
mi	me	ci	us
ti	you (informal	vi	you (informal
gli	him, it	loro	them
le	her, it	loro	them
Le	you (formal	Loro	you (formal

Lui mi ha mandato un regala dalla Francia.

He (has sent me a gift from France.

Possessive Pronouns (Pronomi Possessivi and Possessive Adjectives (Adjettive Possessivi

Possessive Adjectives	Possessive Pronouns	Masculine		Feminine	
		Singular	Plural	Singular	Plural
my	mine	il mio	i miei	la mia	le mie
your (fam.	yours	il tuo	i tuoi	la tua	le tue
your (pol.	yours	il Suo	i Suoi	la Sua	le Sue
his, her , its	hers,his, its	il suo	i suoi	la sua	le sue
our	ours	il nostro	i nostri	la nostra	le nostre
your (fam.	yours	il vostro	i vostri	la vostra	le vostre
your (pol.	yours	il Loro	i Loro	la Loro	le Loro
their	theirs	il loro	i loro	la loro	le loro

Possessive pronouns and possessive adjectives must agree in number and gender with the noun possessed and are identical in form but differ in meaning. They are commonly used with a definite article which is not expressed when translating to English.

Examples:

Possessive adjectives	Possessive Pronouns
Questo è il mio cane.	Questo è il mio.
This is my dog.	This is mine.
Questi sono i miei cani.	Questi sono i miei.
These are my dogs.	These are mine.

The definite article is ommitted only if the possessed noun is a specific relative.

| Mia madre è gentile. | My mother is kind. |
| Mio figlio è molto intelligente. | My son is very kind. |

Demonstrative Pronouns (Pronomi Dimostrativi

Demonstrative pronouns point to a person or thing. They have the same forms as demonstrative adjectives.

Here are the demonstrative pronouns in Italian:

	Singolare	Singular	Plurale	Plural
Masculine	questo	this/this one	questi	these/these ones
Feminine	questa	this/this one	queste	these/these ones
Masculine	quello	that/that one	quelli	those/those ones
Feminine	quella	that/that one	quelle	those/those ones

Examples:

Questa è la tua penna.	This is your pen.
Questo è il mio padre.	That is my father.
Queste sono le tue zie.	These are your aunts.

Chapter 14: Adjectives (Aggettivi)

Like the words they describe, adjectives are masculine or feminine and they are declined according to the number and gender of the noun or pronoun they modify.

Italian adjectives have attributive and predicative functions.

An adjective performs the attributive function when it is used to describe a noun:

Examples:

una casa grande	a big house
un bambino alto	a tall child
un leader onesto	an honest leader

An adjective performs a predicative function if it is used to describe a noun with the use of a linking verb.

La casa è grande.	The house is big.
Il bambino è alto.	The child is tall.
Il leader è intelligente.	The leader is intelligent.

Placement of Adjectives

Adjectives are generally placed after the noun they modify.

Giovanni è una persona laboriosa.	Giovanni is a hardworking person.
Lei è una donna meravigliosa.	She is a wonderful woman.
Egli possiede un auto blu .	He owns a blue car.
Il bambino coraggioso inseguito il ladro.	The brave boy chased the thief.

There are notable exceptions to the above rule and they include several commonly-used adjectives. These adjectives typically came before the noun:

nuovo	new
vecchio	old
giovane	young
cattivo	bad
buono	good
bello	beautiful
brutto	ugly
caro	dear
stesso	same
bravo	good, able
piccolo	small, little
grande	large, great
lungo	long
vero	true

Examples:

Vivono in una grande casa.	They live in a big house.
Il lungo viaggio è stato faticoso.	The long ride was tiring.
Suo padre gli ha dato la vecchia auto.	His father gave him the old car.

When an adverb is used to modify the adjective or when making emphasis, the above adjectives may be placed after the noun they modify.

Ha venduto una macchina molto vecchia.	He sold a very old car.

Declension of Adjectives

Adjectives must agree in number and gender with the word they modify. The following rules govern the declension of adjectives:

Adjectives ending with –o

Adjectives ending in –o takes four endings.

	Masculine	Feminine
Singular	-o	-a
Plural	-i	-e

Lento -> slow

	Masculine	Feminine
Singular	lento	lenta
Plural	lenti	lente

Examples:

la <u>lunga</u> strada	the long road
l'<u>orgoglioso</u> padre	the proud father
gli uomini <u>generosi</u>	the generous men
le <u>nuove</u> case	the new houses

Adjectives ending with –e

Adjectives that end in -e take the same ending in the singular masculine and feminine form but change to –i in the plural.

Example:

Dolce -> sweet

	Singular	Plural
Masculine	dolce	dolce
Feminine	dolci	dolci

Egli è un uomo <u>forte</u>.

He is a strong man.

Lei è un testimone ostile.

She is a hostile witness.

Quelli erano tempi entusiasmanti per i bambini.

Those were exciting time for the children.

Adjectives ending with –ista

Adjectives ending in –ista has three different endings

	Masculine	Feminine
Singular	-sta	-sta
Plural	-sti	-ste

Example:

Egoista -> selfish

	Masculine	Feminine
Singular	egoista	egoista
Plural	egoisti	egoiste

Examples:

un padre ottimista	an optimistic father
una signora molto pessimista	a very pessimistic lady
dei padri ottimista	some optimistic fathers
le signore ottimista	the optimistic ladies

Adjectives ending with –one

Adjectives that end in –one take on three endings.

	Masculine	Feminine
Singular	-one	-ona
Plural	-oni	-one

Example:

Chiacchierone -> mouthy

	Masculine	Feminine
Singular	chiacchierone	chiacchierona
Plural	chiacchieroni	chiacchierone

il ragazzo pasticcione	the bungling boy
una donna pasticcione	a bungling woman
i ragazzi pasticcioni	the bungling boys
le ragazze pasticcioni	the bungling girls

Chapter 15: Invariable adjectives (aggettivi invariabili)

Invariable adjectives retain their form regardless of the number and gender of the words they modify.

Pari (equal, impair (unequal, and dispari) (odd)

The following colors: blu (blue, marrone) (brown, rosa) (pink, and viola) (violet)

Adjectives formed from adverbial expressions:

dabbene (honest, perbene (respectable, and dappoco) (insignificant)

New compound adjectives using the prefix "anti": antiruggine (anti-rust) antifurto (anti-theft)

Adjectives that are declined under similar rules for nouns of the same ending:

Adjectives which end with –io

Adjectives which end with "-co" and "-go"

Irregular Adjectives

When they are placed before a noun, these four common adjectives take irregular forms:

buono	good
bello	beautiful
santo	holy/saint
grande	big/great

Buono

The adjective "buono" is declined in accordance with the following rules:

If the noun modified is masculine:

Singular	Plural	If the adjective comes before
buono	buoni	Nouns that begin with s+z and foreign-derived nouns starting with gn, pn, ps, i, x or y+vowel
buon	buoni	Nouns that begin with consonant or vowel other than those that require the adjective "buono"

Examples:

un buono ragazzo	a good boy
gli buoni tempi	the good times
degli buoni agricoltori	some good farmers

If the noun is feminine:

Singular	Plural	If the adjective is placed before:
buona	buone	Nouns that begin with a consonant
buon	buone	Nouns that begin with a vowel

Examples:

una buona vita	a good life
delle buone madri	some good mothers
una buon attrice	a good actress
le buone attrici	the good actresses

Bello

To agree with the noun it modifies, "belo" changes its ending in accordance with the rules applied to definite articles:

If the noun that comes after it is masculine:

Singular	Plural	
bell'	begli	if the noun starts with a vowel
bello	begli	if the noun starts with s+consonant, z, ps, gn, pn, x, i, y+vowel
bel	bei	if the noun starts with a consonant except when "bello" or "begli" are required

Examples:

il bel bambino (a handsome child, un bello specchio (a beautiful mirror,

When the noun it modifies is feminine:

Singular	Plural	If placed before
bell'	belle	nouns starting with a vowel
bella	belle	nouns starting with a consonant

Examples:

una bella mattina, delle belle flori, mia bell' amica, le belle amiche

Santo

The adjective "santo" changes its ending to conform with the word it precedes in accordance with these rules:

If "santo" comes before a masculine noun:

Singular	Plural	If the adjective comes before
santo	santi	Nouns begining with s+consonant, z, pn, gn, ps, y+vowel, i, or x.
san	santi	Nouns beginning with a vowel or a consonant unless "santo" has to be used

Examples:

San Pellegrino, Santi Paolo e Stefano, San Pietro

If "santo" comes before a feminine noun:

Singular	Plural	If the adjectives comes before
santa	santé	nouns beginninng with a consonant
sant'	santé	nouns beginning with a vowel

Examples:

Santa Teresa, Sant' Emiliana, el Sante Teresa e Emiliana

Grande

To agree with the noun that comes after it, "grande" changes its ending using the following rules:

If grande precedes a masculine noun, the following forms are used:

Singular	Plural	If grande comes before:
Grand'/grande	Grandi	Nouns that begin with a vowel
Gran/grande	Grandi	Nouns that begin with a consonant except when only" grande" should be used
Grande	Grandi	Nouns that begin with s+consonant, z, I, x, gn, ps, pn, or y+vowel.

Adjectives Ending in –e

trustworthy	affidabile
friendly	amichevole
bold/daring	audace
skilled	capace
confidential	confidenziale
courteous/kind	cortese
weak	debole
difficult	difficile
hardworking	diligente
amusing	divertente
sweet	dolce

excellent	eccellente
elegant	elegante
exciting	emozionante
enormous, huge	enorme
easy	facile
happy	felice
formal	formale
strong	forte
lucky	fortunate
futile	futile
kind	gentile
young	giovane
big	grande
important	importante
independent	indipendente
informal	informale
intelligent	intelligente
interesting	interessante
useless	inutile
better	megliore
original	originale
hostile	ostile
patient	paziente
worst	peggiore
dangerous	pericolose
persistent	persistente
pleasant	piacevole
careful/cautious	prudente
childish	puerile
punctual	puntuale
smelly	puzzolente
rude	scortese

simple	semplice
sensitive	sensibile
unfavorable	sfavorevole
gaudy	sgargiante
sincere	sincere
soft	soffice
active	sportive
terrible	terribile
sad	triste
humble	umile
useful	utile
fast	veloce

Adjectives Endings in −o

wet	agnato
short	aasso
sour	acido
hungry	affamato
aggressive	aggressivo
happy	allegro
tall	alto
other	altro
wide	ampio
bored	annoiato
anxious	ansioso
ancient	antico
mean	antipatico
old	anziano
open	aperto
angry	arrabbiato
attentive	attento

stingy	avaro
beautiful	bello
capable/talented	bravo
ugly	brutto
funny	buffo
good	buono
stormy	burrascoso
calm	calmo
pretty	carino
expensive	caro
bad	cattivo
light	chiaro
closed	chiuso
colorful	colorato
glad	content
courageous	coraggioso
expensive	costoso
curious	curioso
delicious	delizioso
disappointed	deluso
right (direction	destroy
dynamic	dinamico
straight	diritto
carefree	disinvolto
dishonest	disonesto
destroyed	distrutto
hard	duro
foreign	estero
insincere	falso
crushed, shattered	frantumato
fresh	fresco
hasty	frettoloso

fried	fritto
shrewd	furbo
jealous	geloso
generous	generoso
right	giusto
fat	grasso
raw	grezzo
broken	ifranto
busy	impegnato
naive	ingenuo
light	leggero
slow	lento
long	lungo
luxurious	lussurioso
thin	magro
sick	malatto
half	mezzo
mixed	misto
dead	morto
boring/tedious	noioso
well-known	noto
new	nuovo
cloudy	nuvoloso
busy	occupato
odious, detestable, hateful	odioso
honest	onesto
proud	orgoglioso
obstinate	ostinato
weird	pazzesco
crazy	pazzo
sinful	peccaminoso
worse	peggio

full	peino
perfect	perfetto
small	piccolo
lazy	pigro
rainy	piovoso
poor	povero
favorite	preferito
first	primo
deep	profondo
next	prossimo
daily	quotidiano
religious	religioso
rich	ricco
noisy	rumoroso
rough	ruvido
salty	salato
safe	salvo
wrong	sbagliato
silly	sciocco
dark	scuro
dry	secco
serious	serio
silky	setoso
strict	severo
cheeky	sfacciato
exhausted	sfinito
unlucky	sfortunato
secure	sicuro
nice	simpatico
left	sinistro
slender	slanciato
slim	snello

sunny	soleggiato
scared	spaventato
hopeful	speranzoso
shameless	spudorato
tired	stanco
same	stesso
stressed	stressato
studious	studioso
stupid	stupid
shy	timido
calm, quiet	tranquillo
last	ultimo
humid	umido
old	vecchio
true	vero
alive	vivo
empty	vuoto
quiet	zitto

Adjectives Ending in –ista

selfish	egoista
enthusiastic	entusiasta
optimistic	ottimista
pessimistic	pessimista

Chapter 16: Verbs

Verbs describe action, state of being, or occurrence. In Italian, verbs serve the following functions:

Verbs indicate the doer of the action.

The doer of the action can be masculine (io, tu, lui), feminine (lei), a group of either masculine or feminine, or a mix of both genders,

Verbs indicate how the action happens.

The Italian language has several moods with different forms and functions: the indicative mood (indicative, the subjunctive (conguintivo), the imperative (imperative), infinitive (infinitive), conditional (condizionale), the participle (participio), and the gerund (gerundio) mood.

A verb tells when an action happens.

Verbs have moods and tenses.

A verb specifies the form or type of action taking place.

Italian verb forms can be active (transitive or intransitive), passive, and reflexive.

A majority of Italian verbs have simiar endings and follow three distinct patterns: -are, -ere, and –ire. They are grouped and conjugated in accordance with their endings in the infinitive form.

Here are examples of verbs under the 3 Verb Groups:

The −are verbs:

andare	to go
arbitare	to live
arrivare	to arrive
dare	to give
amare	to love
inziare	to begin
fare	to do/make
indossare	to wear
comprare	to buy
amare	to love
mangiare	to eat
giocare	to play
studiare	to study
circare	to look for
camminare	to walk
ballare	to dance
pensare	to think
guardare	to watch/guard
chiamare	to call
cantare	to sing
portare	to carry
invitare	to invite
lavorare	to work
ordinare	to order
lasciare	to leave
avere bisogno di	to need
imparare	to learn
cambiare	to change
viaggiare	to travel
cucinare	to cook

The −ere verbs:

vedere	to see
dire	to say
leggere	to read
temere	to fear
saltare	to jump
scrivere	to write
vivere	to live
credere	to believe
volere	to want
sapere	to know
dovere	to owe
mettere	to put
chiedere	to ask for
conoscere	to know
vendere	to sell
piacere	to like
bere	to drink

The –ire Verbs

salire	to get in
aprire	to open
dormire	to sleep
venire	to come
seguire	to follow
salire	to go up
sentire	to hear
finire	to finish
servire	to serve
preferire	to prefer
pulire	to clean
morire	to die
colpire	to hit

Chapter 17: Verb Conjugations

Italian verbs change their form to signify who or what is performing the action and when. Verbs belonging to –are, -ere, and –ire groups take on endings indicated for each verb class.

To conjuge regular verbs, just follow these steps:

Get the verb stem by dropping the –are, -ere, or –ire ending.

For example, to get the stem of the verb amare, drop the –are ending to come up with "am".

Add the indicated ending based on the –are verbs conjugation table.

For instance, the ending for the first person in the present indicative tense is -o. To express I love, you'll say "Io amo (am+o)". To say" I love you" , say "Io ti amo".

The Present Tense (Il Tempo Presente)

The present tense is used to denote action in the present indicate (she reads). In addition, the present tense of Italian verbs is also used to signify the present progressive tense (she is reading). The subject pronoun may be omitted because the verb's subject is already indicated by the verb's ending.

Conjugation tables for the Present Tense

-are verbs

Subject	English	-are verbs
io	I	-o
tu	You	-i
lui/lei	he/she	-a
noi	We	-iamo
voi	you	-ate
Loro	they/you (formal)	-ano

Hence, to conjugate lavorare (to work

Subject	English	lavorare
io	I	lavoro
tu	you	lavori
lui/lei	he/she	lavora
noi	we	lavoriamo
voi	you	lavorate
Loro	they/you (formal)	lavorano

Sentences:

Lavoro a Intel. (I work at Intel.)

Lavoriamo da Lunedi a Venerdì ogni sett.

(We work from Monday to Friday every week.)

-ere verbs

Subject	English	-ere verbs
io	I	-o
tu	you	-i
lui/lei	he/she	-e
noi	we	-iamo
voi	you	-ete
loro	they/you (formal)	-ono

To conjugate leggere (to read):

Subject	English	leggere
io	I	leggo
tu	You	leggi
lui/lei	he/she	legge
noi	We	leggiamo
voi	You	leggete
Loro	they/you (formal)	leggono

Sentences:

Io leggo libri nei finesettimana. (I read books on weekends.)

Raramente leggono i giornali. (They rarely read newspapers)

-ire verbs

Subject	English	-ire verbs
Io	I	-o
Tu	you	-i
lui/lei	he/she	-e
Noi	we	-iamo
Voi	you	-ite
Loro	they/you (formal)	-ono

To conjugate aprire (to open)

Subject	English	aprire
io	I	aprio
tu	you	apri
lui/lei	he/she	apre
noi	we	apriamo
voi	you	aprite
Loro	they/you (formal)	aprono

Apro la porta per farli entrare. (I open the door to let them in.)

Le guardie aprono il cancello del centro commerciale ogni alle 10 del mattino.

(The guards open the mall's gate every 10:00 in the morning.)

The Verbs Avere and Essere

The verbs avere (to have) and essere (to be) are auxiliary verbs, which help form compound tenses. In addition, essere is used in forming the passive voice.

The verbs avere and essere have irregular conjuctions:

Present Tense (avere)

Subject	English	avere
io	I	Ho
tu	You	Hai
lui/lei	he/she	Ha
noi	We	abbiamo
voi	You	avete
Loro	they/you (formal)	hanno

Present Tense (avere)

Subject	English	essere
io	I	sono
tu	You	sei
lui/lei	he/she	è
noi	We	siamo
voi	You	siete
Loro	they/you (formal)	sono

Many are confused on what auxiliary verb to use when forming compound verbs. A simple approach is to check whether the verb is transitive or intransitive. Transitive verbs require a direct object and take the auxiliary verb avere. Intransive verbs, on the other hand, take essere.

Examples:

Avere:	Ho visitato una riserva natural.	I visited a wildlife sanctuary.
Essere:	Marco è andato alla Francia.	Marco has gone to France.

Past Tense - essere

ero	I was
eri	you were
era	he/she was
eravamo	we were
eravate	you were
erano	they were

Future tense - essere

sarò	I will be
sarai	you will be
sarà	he/she will be
saremo	we will be
sarete	you will be
saranno	they will be

Past Tense – avere

avevo	I had
avevi	you had
aveva	he/she had
avevamo	we had
avevate	you had
avevano	they had

Future Tense – avere

avrò	I will have
avrai	you will have
avrà	he/she will have
avremo	we will have
avrete	you will have
avranno	they will have

The past participle forms of avere and essere are as follows:

Infinitive	past participle
avere	avuto
essere	stato

The Past Participle Form (Il Participio Passato)

Past participles are formed by dropping the regular verb endings and adding the indicated ending for each verb group.

Verbs	Past Participle Ending	Examples	
-are verbs	-ato	lavorare	lavorato
-ere verbs	-uto	leggere	legguto
-ire verbs	-ito	aprire	aprito

The Present Perfect (Il Passato Prossimo)

The passato prossimo is a compound tense that indicates:

facts or actions that were completed in the recent past

Example:

I submitted my homework yesterday.

We watched a movie a month ago.

actions that happened in the past but continue to have ties in the present

Example:

We have not submitted our homework yet.

I have been to Switzerland twice.

The passato prossimo consists of two verbs:

Present indicative form of essere or avere + past participle of the main verb

Examples:

Ho mangiato un sandwich di pollo. I have eaten a chicken sandwich.

Siamo andati alla festa ieri sera. We went to the party last night.

Chapter 18: The Simple Future Tense (Il Futuro Semplice)

The simple future tense is used to indicate actions that will occur in the future. The three regular verb groups take on similar endings in the simple future. There is, however, a minor difference in how they are conjugated. The –ere and –ire verb forms are conjugated by dropping the final –e and adding the indicated endings for the simple future. The –are verbs are conjugated by dropping the –are, adding –er, and the indicated endings.

Here are the verb endings for the simple future tense:

Subject	English	Endings
Io	I	ò
Tu	You	ai
lui/lei	he/she	à
Noi	We	emo
Voi	You	ete
Loro	they/you (formal)	anno

Examples:

-are verbs:

pensare (to think)	pens +er + verb ending
Io penserò.	I will think.
Tu penserai.	You will think.
Lei penserà.	She will think.
Noi penseremo.	We will think.
Voi penserete.	You (plural will think.)
Loro penseranno.	They will think.

-ere verbs

scrivere (to write)	scriver + verb ending
Io scriverò.	I will write.
Tu scriverai.	You will write.
Lui scriverà.	He will write.
Noi scriveremo.	We will write.
Voi scriverete.	You (plural will write.)
Loro scriveranno.	They will write.

-ire verbs

pulire (to clean)	pulir + verb ending
Io pulirò.	I will clean.
Tu pulirai.	You will clean.
Lui pulirà.	He will clean.
Noi puliremo.	We will clean.
Voi pulirete.	You will clean.
Loro puliranno.	They will clean.

The Reflexive Verbs (I Verbi Riflessivi)

Reflexive verbs are used when the doer (subject and the receiver) (object of the action) are the same. English has less need for reflexive verbs than Italian because the subject and the object are easily identifiable. For instance, if you say "I take a bath", it's obvious that it's yourself that has taken a bath. This is not so in many Italian reflexive verbs. When using a reflexive verb in Italian, you have to use the appropriate reflexive pronoun before the verb.

Here are the reflexive pronouns:

mi	myself
ti	yourself
si	himself, herself, itself, yourself (formal)
si	themselves, yourselves (formal)
ci	ourselves
vi	yourselves

This is how the subject pronouns match with reflexive pronouns:

io	mi
tu	ti
lui	si
lei	si
Lei	si
noi	ci
voi	vi
loro	si
Loro	si

There are many Italian verbs with reflexive forms and they are easy to recognize as they end with –si.

Here are common reflexive verbs:

to feel	sentirsi
to get angry	arrabbiarsi
to go to sleep/fall asleep	addormentarsi
to comb one's hair	pettinarsi
to sit down	sedersi
to get up	alzarsi
to greet each other	salutarsi
to be bored	annoiarsi
to wash oneself	lavarsi
to dry off	asciugarsi
to wake up	svegliarsi
to put clothes on	mettersi
to be called	chiamarsi
to put makeup on	truccarsi
to enjoy oneself	divertirsi
to worry (about)	preoccuparsi (di)
to shave oneself	farsi la barba
to read the paper	leggere il giornale
to bathe onself	farsi il bagno
to get dressed	vestirsi
to stop	fermarsi
to prepare oneself for	preparasi per (+ inf)
to begin	mettersi a (+ inf)

To form a reflexive sentence or clause, you will need the following:

subject+reflexive pronoun+conjugated verb

To conjugate reflexive verbs, drop the −si ending and use the endings for −are, -ere, and −ire verbs.

For example, to conjugate "pettinarsi" (to comb one's hair) in the present tense, drop −si and use the endings for the verb −are. Thus:

(io) mi pettino

(tu) ti pettini

(lui) si pettina

(noi) ci pettiniamo

(voi) vi pettinate

(loro/Loro) si pettinano

To conjugate mettersi (to put clothes on, drop the −si ending and use the endings for the verb −ere. Hence:

(io mi metto

(tu ti metti

(lui si mette

(noi ci mettiamo

(voi vi mettete

(loro/Loro si mettono

To conjugate sentirsi t(to feel, drop the –si ending and use the endings for the verb –ire. Thus:

(io mi sento

(tu ti senti

(lui si sente

(noi ci sentiamo

(voi vi sentiti

(loro/Loro si sentono

Sentences:

Mi pettino i capelli.	I comb my hair.
Mi sento triste per le vittime.	I feel sad for the victims.

Chapter 19: The Adverbs (Gli Avverbi)

An adverb modifies an adjective, a verb, or another adverb. Adverbs answer the questions when, where, how, and how often. While English adverbs are usually formed by adding –ly to adjectives, many Italian adverbs are formed by affixing –mente to the adjective's feminine form. Adjectives ending in either –re or –le drop the final –e before adding –mente. Adverbs are invariable words.

Examples:

Adjective	Adverb
alta (high)	altamente (highly)
semplice (simple)	simplicemente (simply)
vera (true)	veramente (truly)
gentile (kind)	gentilmente (kindly)
regolare (regular)	regolarmente(regularly)

Placement of Adverbs

Adverbs which modify an adjective are placed before the adjective.

Lui è un uomo <u>molto</u> generoso. (He is a very generous man.)

When it modifies a verb, the adverb usually comes after the verb.

Il vecchio uomo cammina <u>lentamente</u>. (The old man walks slowly.)

When it refers to a verb in a compound tense, some adverbs may come between the auxiliary verb and the conjugated verb.

Non hanno <u>mai</u> mangiato piatti di maiale. (They have never eaten pork dishes.)

When an adverb modifies another adverb, adverbs of quantity come before over adverbs.

Solito dormo molto tardi durante i fine settiman.

(I usually sleep quite late during weekends.)

List of Adverbs

Adverbs of Time

dopo	after
già	already,
tosto	at once
dapprima	at the outset, at first
mai	ever
sempre	ever
infine	finally

tardi	late
adesso	now
ebbene	nowadays
oggigiorno	nowadays
sovente	often
spesso	often
presto	soon, early
ancora	still, yet
l'indomani	the day after
allora	then
stamattina	this morning
stasera	this night
oggi	today
domani	tomorrow
stanotte	tonight
quando	when

Adverbs of Place

sopra	above, on top
distante	away
lontano	away
davanti	before
prima	before
sotto	below, downstairs
ovunque	everywere
dappertutto	everywhere
ne	from here/there
oltre	further
lì	here
qui/qua	here
vi	here/there

vicino	near
fuori	outside, outdoors
oltremare	overseas
ci	there
laggiù	there
là	there
dove	where
dentro	within, inside

Adverbs of Quantity

circa	about, approximately
quasi	almost, nearly
quanto	as many, as much
abbastanza	enough
meno	less
poco	little
più	more
solo	only
così	so
oltremodo	too, exceedingly
troppo	too, too much
molto	very, very much, quite

Interrogative Adverbs

come	how
quanto	how much/many
quando	when
dove	where
perché	why
come mai	why

131

Adverbs of Manner

soprattutto	above all, especially
male	badly
perbene	duly
anche	even, too
come	like, such as
forte	loudly, aloud
altrimenti	otherwise
piano	silently
adagio	slowly, carefully
così	so, thus
presto	soon, quickly
bene	well
volentieri	willingly

Adverbs of Affirmation/Negation

davvero	absolutely, really, indeed
appena	barely, hardly
sicuro	certainly, sure
certo	certainly, sure
neanche	even not
forse	maybe, possibly
ne	neither
giammai	never
mai	never
non	no
no	not
sì	yes

Chapter 20: Prepositions (Prepozioni)

Prepositions connect words and clauses and are invariable. They express directions, conditions, and specifications. Italian prepositions may be classified into two categories: simple prepositions and articulated prepositions. Articulated prepositions are simple prepositions, which are used with a definite article.

Simple Prepositions (Preposizioni Semplici)

a	at, to, in
con	with
da	from, by, since
per	for, per, via
in	in, within
tra	between, from among
fra	between, in
di	of, from, at
su	on, up,, upward
verso	about, approximately
secondo	according to
dopochè	after
inverso	against
contro	against, in exchange for
avanti	before
dietro	behind
indietro	behind
sotto	below, under
oltre	beyond, further
durante	during, while
davanti	formerly, before, ahead

malgrado	in spite of
dopo	later, after, soon
presso	nearby
in avanti	onwards, forward
fuori	out(side
dentro	within, in, into
senza	without

Examples:

Mia madre andò a New York.	My mother went to New York.
Vive in Francia.	She lives in France.
La sua casa si trova tra due edifici alti.	His house is between two tall buildings.
Questo dono è per Irma.	This gift is for Irma.
Il bambino sta giocando con i suoi giocattoli.	The boy is playing with his toys.
E ' da Roma.	He is from Rome.

Articulated Prepositions (Preposizioni Articolate

A preposition may at times precede a definite article. In such instances, the prepositions a, da, su, in, col, and di will contract with the definite article to form one word known as articulated preposition. Other prepositions may also precede a definite article but will remain separate. Here is a table showing articulated prepositions:

	il	lo/L'	la/l'	i	gli	le
di	del	dello/ dell'	della/ dell'	dei	degli	delle
a	al	allo/all'	alla/all'	ai	agli	alle
da	dal	dallo/ dall'	dalla/ dall'	dai	dagli	dale
in	nel	nello/ nell'	nella/ nell'	nei	negli	nelle

su	sul	sullo/s ull'	sulla/ sull'	sui	sugli	sulle
con	col	collo/ coll'	colla/ coll'	coi	cogli	colle
per	pel			pei		

a+il	Io vado <u>al</u> museo.	I'm going to the museum.
di+la	Chiuse la porta <u>della</u> macchina.	She closed the door of the car.
di+il	Il mio vicino di casa nostra è il conducente del bus.	My neighbor is the driver of the bus.

Chapter 21: Vocabulary

The Family (La Famiglia)

the dad	il papa
the mom	la mamma
the father	il padre
the mother	la madre
the grandpa	il nonno
the grandma	la nonna
the grandparents	i nonni
the uncle	lo zio
the aunt	la zia
the husband	il marito
the wife	la moglie
the brother	il fratello
the sister	la sorella
the father-in-law	il suocero
the mother-in-law	la suocera
the brother-in-law	il cognato
the sister-in-law	la cognata
the son-in-law	il genero
the daughter-in-law	la nuora
the nephew	il nipote
the niece	la nipote
the cousins	i cugini, le cugine
the boyfriend	il ragazzo
the girlfriend	la ragazza
the son	il figlio
the daughter	la figlia
the fiancé	il fidanzato, la fidanzata

The Professions (Le Professioni)

the barber	il barbiere
the librarian	il bibliotecario, la bibliotecaria
the waiter	il cameriere, la cameriera
the cashier	il cassiere, la cassiera
the chef	il cuoco
the boss	il direttore
the doctor	il dottore, la dottoressa
the carpenter	il falegname
the judge	il giudice
the construction worker	il lavoratore edile
the butcher	il macellaio
the mechanic	il meccanico
the mason	il muratore
the hair dresser	il parrucchiere, la parrucchiera
the police officer	il poliziotto
the firefighter	il pompiere
the mail carrier	il postino
the president	il presidente
the professor	il professore, la professoressa
the programmer	il programmatore
the accountant	il ragioniere
the secretary	il segretario, la segretaria
the computer technician	il tecnico del computer
the veterinarian	il veterinario
the reporter	il/la cronista
the dentist	il/la dentista
the farmer	l'agricoltore
the coach	l'allenatore
the artist	l'artista
the athlete	l'atleta

the actor	l'attore
the lawyer	l'avvocato
the nurse	l'infermiere, l'infermiera
the engineer	l'ingegnere
the writer	lo scrittore, la scrittrice
the business person	l'uomo d'affari

Foods (Cibi)

the appetizer	l'antipasto
the beans	i fagioli
the beef	la carne di manzo
the beet	la barbabietola
the turkey	il tacchino
the chicken	il pollo
the fish (cooked	il pesce (cotto
the pork	il maiale
the butter	il burro
the cheese	il formaggio
the dessert	il dolce
the egg	l'uovo
the fish (cooked	il pesce (cotto
the flour	la farina
the french fries	le patatine fritte
the sandwich	il panino
the hamburger	l'hamburger
the hotdog	l'hotdog
the popcorn	i popcorn
the honey	il miele
the jam	la marmellata
the jelly	la gelatina (di frutta
the peanut butter	il burro di noccioline

the ketchup	il ketchup
the mayonnaise	la maionese
the milk	il latte
the juice	il succo
the water	l'acqua
the salad	l'insalata
the soup	la minestra
the mustard	la mostarda
the nut	la noce
the candy	la caramella
the raisin	l'uvetta
the peanut	la nocciolina
the sugar	lo zucchero
the flour	la farina

Fruits (Frutta)

apricot	albicocca
pineapple	ananas
watermelon	anguria
orange	arancia
banana	banana
cherry	ciliegia
strawberry	fragola
kiwi	kiwi
raspberry	lampone
lemon	limone
mandarin	mandarino
black cherry	marena
apple	mela
pomegranate	melagrana
melon	melone

blueberry	mirtillo
coconut	noce di cocco
pear	pera
peach	pesca
grapefruit	pompelmo
grape	uva

Vegetables (la verdure)

garlic	aglio
carrot	carota
onion	cipolla
lettuce	lattuga
aubergine	melanzana
tomato	pomodoro
parsley	prezzemolo
chicory	radicchio
radish	ravanello
celery	sedano
pumpkin	zucca
zucchini	zucchini

Animals (Gli Animali)

the dog	il cane
the kangaroo	il canguro
the beaver	il castoro
the horse	il cavallo
the deer	il cervo
the rabbit	il coniglio
the puppy	il cucciolo
the kitten	il gattino

the cat	il gatto
the gorilla	il gorilla
the llama	il lama
the leopard	il leopard
the wolf	il lupo
the panda	il panda
the fish	il pesce
the penguin	il pinguino
the rat	il ratto
the rhino	il rinoceronte
the mouse	il topo
the whale	la balena
the goat	la capra
the hyena	la iena
the sheep	la pecora
the monkey	la scimmia
the tiger	la tigre
the fox	la volpe
the zebra	la zebra
the elephant	l'elefante
the hippopotamus	l'ippopotamo
the chimpanzee	lo scimpanzé
the squirrel	lo scoiattolo
the bear	l'orso

Sports (Gli Sport)

badminton	(il badminton
baseball	(il baseball
soccer	(il calcio
cycling	(il ciclismo
cricket	(il cricket

football	(il football americano
golf	(il golf
swimming	(il nuoto
ping pong	(il ping pong
rugby	(il rugby
tennis	(il tennis
horseback riding	(l' equitazione
hockey	(l' hockey
basketball	(la pallacanestro
team handball	(la pallamano
volleyball	(la pallavolo
the game	la partita
the team	la squadra
sporting event	l'evento sportivo

Countries (Paesi)

Argentina	l'Argentina
Asia	l'Asia
Australia	l'Australia
Belgium	il Belgio
Brazil	il Brasile
Canada	il Canada
Chile	il Cile
China	la Cina
England	l'Inghilterra
France	la Francia
Germany	la Germania
India	l'India
Iran	l'Iran
Iraq	l'Iraq
Ireland	l'Irlanda

Israel	Israele
Japan	il Giappone
Lebanon	il Libano
Mexico	il Messico
New Zealand	la Nuova Zelanda
Panama	Panama
Philippines	le Filippine
Portugal	il Portogallo
Russia	la Russia
Spain	la Spagna
Sweden	la Svezia
Switzerland	la Svizzera
United States	li Stati Uniti
Uruguay	l'Uruguay
Vietnam	il Vietnam

Continents (Continenti)

Africa	l'Africa
Antarctica	l'Antartica
Asia	l'Asia
Australia	l'Australia
Europe	l'Europa
North America	l'America del Nord
South America	l'America del Sud

Vehicles (Veicoli)

the truck	il camion
the taxi	il taxi / il tassì
the train	il treno
the bicycle	la bicicletta
the car	la macchina

the motorcycle	la motocicletta
the airplane	l'aeroplano
the helicopter	l'elicottero

Appliances (Elettrodomestici)

the freezer	il congelatore
the iron	il ferro
the oven	il forno
the fridge	il frigorífero
the blender	il frullatore
the microwave	il microonde
the toaster	il tostapane
the dishwasher	la lavastoviglie
the washer	la lavatrice
the dryer	l'asciugatrice
the water heater	lo scaldaacqua

The Weather (Il Meteo)

hot	caldo
it's sunny	c'è il sole
it's windy	c'è vento
cold	freddo
the sun	il sole
the thermometer	il termometro
the tornado	il tornado
the fog	la nebbia
the snow	la neve
the cloud	la nuvola
the rain	la pioggia
the temperature	la temperatura

the flood	l'inondazione
the humidity	l'umidità
the hurricane	l'uragano
foggy	nebbioso
cloudy	nuvoloso
windy	ventoso

Nature (Natura)

the flower	il fiore
the river	il fiume
the garden	il giardino
the lake	il lago
the sea	il mare
the soil	il suolo
the mountain range	la catena montuosa
the plant	la pianta
the shore	la riva
the cliff	la rupe
the tree	l'albero
the waterfalls	le cascate
the herb	le erbe
the mountains	le montagne
the grass (lawn	l'erba (il prato
the weed	l'erbaccia
the ocean	l'oceano
the garden (vegetable	l'orto

Furniture (i mobili

the garbage can	il bidone della spazzatura
the sofa	il divano

the bed	il letto
the piano	il pianoforte
the table	il tavolo
the armchair	la poltrona
the desk	la scrivania
the chair	la sedia

Outside (Fuori

the window	el finestrino
the chimney	il camino
the bush	il cespuglio
the garage	il garage
the sidewalk	il marciapiede
the brick	il mattone
the wall	il muro
the porch	il portico
the lawn	il prato
the roof	il tetto
the driveway	il vialetto (del garage
the door	la porta
the patio	la terrazza

Places to Visit

Il centro commercial	the shopping center
L'agenzia di viaggio	the travel agency
Il centro città	the town center
Il ristorante	the restaurant
La stazione di polizia	the police station
Il parco	the park
Il monument	the monument
Il centro storico	the historic center

I bagni pubblici	the public restrooms
L'ospedale	the hospital
Il municipio	the town hall
La periferia	the suburb
Il bar	the bar

Conclusion

I hope this book was able to help you to communicate confidently and accurately in the Italian language.

It's time for you to take your learning to the higher level by taking up advanced language courses, reading Italian books and novels, watching Italian movies, and speaking regularly to a native Italian speaker.

I wish you the best of luck!

To your success,

Henry Ray

Printed in Great Britain
by Amazon